DOMESTIC DOGS

CHIHUAHUAS

by Susan H. Gray

Published in the United States of America by The Child's World®
PO Box 326 • Chanhassen, MN 55317-0326
800-599-READ • www.childsworld.com

PHOTO CREDITS

© Amy Sancetta/Associated Press: 25
© DLILLC/Corbis: 9, 11
© Gari Wyn Williams/Alamy: 29
© Garry Gay/Alamy: 21
© IPS Co., Ltd./Beateworks/Corbis: 15
© iStockphoto.com/Nicole Weiss: cover, 1
© John Lund/Getty Images: 23
© Juniors Bildarchiv/Alamy: 13
© Richard Levine / Alamy: 27
© Ryuichi Sato/Getty Images: 17
© SuperStock, Inc./SuperStock: 19

ACKNOWLEDGMENTS

The Child's World®: Mary Berendes, Publishing Director;
Katherine Stevenson, Editor

Content Adviser: Lynnie Bunten, President,
Chihuahua Rescue and Transport

The Design Lab: Kathleen Petelinsek, Design and Page Production

LIBRARY OF CONGRESS CATALOGING-IN-PUBLICATION DATA

Chihuahuas / by Susan H. Gray.
    p. cm. — (Domestic dogs)
Includes bibliographical references and index.
ISBN 1-59296-773-6 (library bound : alk. paper)
1. Chihuahua (Dog breed)—Juvenile literature. I. Title. II. Series.
SF429.C45G633 2007
636.76—dc22   2006022636

Table of Contents

NAME That DOG!

What tiny dog is loved by millions of people? What dog sometimes wears a little coat? **What dog might have only one puppy in a litter?** What little dog has big eyes and big ears? If you said "Chihuahua" (chih-WAH-wah), you are correct!

5

Chihuahuas from Chihuahua

No one knows where Chihuahuas first came from. They might have come from an **ancient** kind of dog—the *techichi* (teh-CHEE-chee). People living in Mexico had techichis hundreds of years ago. Techichis were bigger than today's Chihuahuas. They could not bark.

Later, people from Europe and Asia came to the Americas. They brought dogs with them.

United States

Gulf
of
Mexico

Pacific

Ocean

Mexico

Belize

Guatemala

Honduras

El Salvador

Nicaragua

Costa
Rica

The map on the left shows
where Mexico is on Earth.
The map on the right
shows a closer view.

7

The newcomers brought small, hairless dogs from Asia. They brought long-haired dogs from Spain. Chihuahuas might be a mix of techichis and these other dogs.

We might never know where Chihuahuas first came from. But we know how they got their name. About 150 years ago, people found tiny dogs living in Mexico. The dogs lived in Chihuahua, a state next to Texas. People started to call the dogs Chihuahuas. These little dogs quickly became **popular**. Everyone wanted them for pets!

Chihuahuas can be very curious. This one is watching a bird from across the yard.

Very Small Dogs

Chihuahuas are tiny. They are only 6 to 9 inches (15 to 23 centimeters) tall at the shoulder. They weigh only 4 to 6 pounds (2 to 3 kilograms). A house cat weighs twice that much!

Chihuahuas come in many colors. They can be tan, gray, or black—or all three colors. Some have short, smooth coats. Others have long, soft coats. The long coats are either straight or curly. Chihuahuas' tails curl over their backs. Their eyes are dark—sometimes dark red.

This adult Chihuahua is sitting next to a cat. You can see how much smaller the Chihuahua is!

11

Chihuahuas ears are big and stand straight up. Long-haired Chihuahuas have **tufts** of hair on their ears.

All Chihuahuas are born with a soft spot on the forehead. It is called a *molera* (moh-LEHR-uh). The skull bones have not grown together in this spot. As the Chihuahuas get older, these bones grow together. The molera gets hard. On some Chihuahuas, the molera never gets hard. A bump on the head can hurt them badly.

Chihuahuas always seem to stand at attention. Their ears are up. Their eyes are bright. They are ready for anything!

No two Chihuahuas
look alike! Here you
can see four long-haired
Chihuahuas. They all have
different coloring.

No Other Dogs Like Them!

Chihuahuas might be the smallest **breed** of dog. But they are hard to forget! They are full of energy and move quickly. They are also very **loyal**. They stick close to their owners. They watch every move their owners make.

These dogs make great pets. But they must have the right home. They are too small to live in a busy home. They might get stepped on! Sometimes they snap at children. Often, they do not like strangers or other dogs.

This Chihuahua is watching another dog from the safety of his owner's lap.

15

Chihuahuas are not unfriendly. They are just tiny. They must look out for themselves all the time. Children often want to play with them. But playful children can easily hurt a Chihuahua by mistake. Chihuahuas are always watching for danger. They sometimes snap because they are afraid of getting hurt.

Chihuahuas can get used to being around children. They can also make friends with other pets. This works best if the dogs are young. Puppies get used to new things better than adults dogs do.

Chihuahuas love warm spots. They often crawl under blankets or lie in patches of sunshine.

This boy loves his pet Chihuahua. He has learned to play very gently with it.

Tiny Babies

Chihuahuas are so small, they are often called "toy" dogs. Their puppies are small, too. A newborn Chihuahua weighs about as much as a lemon.

Most Chihuahua mothers have only a small litter. Sometimes they have only one puppy. Newborn Chihuahuas have big heads. They have the soft spot on their foreheads. Their ears are small and do not stand up yet.

This mother Chihuahua is watching over her puppies. They are only about two weeks old.

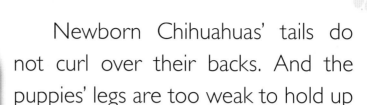

Newborn Chihuahuas grow fast. They almost double their weight in the first week!

Newborn Chihuahuas' tails do not curl over their backs. And the puppies' legs are too weak to hold up their bodies.

As they grow, the puppies get stronger. They begin to run around on their own. But they still need to be **protected**. The soft spot needs to be treated gently. So do the puppies! They can be hurt easily. Some people hang tiny bells on the dogs' necks. The bells tell everyone to walk carefully—a Chihuahua is nearby!

This older Chihuahua puppy is about six weeks old. It is peeking out of a basket.

21

Little Dogs with Big Jobs

Most Chihuahuas are kept as pets. Some make good watchdogs. They bark at strangers. They bark when they think danger is near.

In Texas, a barking Chihuahua saved his owners' lives! Rosco lived in a home with many children. Early one morning, a fire broke out. Everyone was asleep—except Rosco. He barked and barked and woke everyone up. The people saw the flames and escaped. After the fire, the home was gone. But the family was safe. Rosco was everyone's hero.

Chihuahuas bark to warn people or other dogs to stay away. Sometimes they bark to warn their owners of danger!

23

A few Chihuahuas have been in movies or on TV. One Chihuahua became famous for his TV ads. He seemed to "talk" about Mexican food. The little dog became a star. Everyone knew about the Chihuahua that loved tacos.

At least one Chihuahua is even doing police work! Most police dogs are much bigger. They chase people who break the law. They find missing people. They sniff out drugs or stolen goods. One Chihuahua in Ohio is learning to find drugs. Her name is Midge. Midge has a tiny uniform. She even rides on a police motorcycle.

Some owners think their Chihuahuas bark too much. They say their dogs yap.

Here you can see Midge working. She looks at the officer to tell him she smells drugs in a cabinet.

25

Caring for a Chihuahua

The biggest problem with Chihuahuas is their size. People do not see these tiny dogs. They trip over them. Sometimes Chihuahuas get shut in closets. They get trapped in drawers, cars, or even suitcases!

Short-haired Chihuahuas get cold easily. Often, their owners dress them in little jackets. These clothes are not just for fun. They keep the dogs warm.

This Chihuahua's cute sweater also keeps her warm. Her owner is walking her in New York City.

27

Most people want their dogs to get enough exercise. They take them for walks or to the park. But Chihuahuas get plenty of exercise running around the house.

Some Chihuahuas have problems with their knees. Their kneecaps slip out of place. This can hurt and make it hard for the dogs to walk. Other Chihuahuas have a weak **windpipe**. The windpipe can close and keep the dog from breathing. And some Chihuahuas have problems if their molera stays soft.

But most Chihuahuas do not have these problems. They live long, healthy lives. They often live to be 14 or 15. They bring their owners lots of happiness in those years!

Some Chihuahuas like to go for walks on a leash. But pulling against a collar can hurt the dog's windpipe. A **harness** is safer for walks.

This Chihuahua's owner is holding her as they walk through a crowd.

Glossary

ancient (AYN-shunt) Something that is ancient is very old. Chihuahuas might have come from techichis, an ancient kind of dog.

breed (BREED) A breed is a certain type of an animal. Chihuahuas are one of many dog breeds.

harness (HAR-nuss) A harness is a set of bands or belts some animals wear. A harness is safer than a collar for walking a Chihuahua.

litter (LIH-tur) A litter is a group of babies born to one animal at the same time. Chihuahua mothers have very small litters.

loyal (LOY-ul) To be loyal is to be true to something and stand up for it. Chihuahuas are loyal to their owners.

popular (PAH-pyuh-lur) When something is popular, it is liked by lots of people. Chihuahuas are popular dogs.

protected (pruh-TEK-tud) To be protected is to be kept safe. Chihuahuas need to protected so they do not get hurt.

tufts (TUFTS) Tufts are patches of things such as hair, feathers, or grass. Some Chihuahuas have tufts of hair on their ears.

windpipe (WIND-pipe) A windpipe is the tube that carries air to an animal's lungs. Some Chihuahuas have weak windpipes.

To Find Out More

Books to Read

Coile, D. Caroline. *The Chihuahua Handbook*. Hauppauge, NY: Barron's Educational Series, 2003.

Sisco, Roberta. *Chihuahua*. Philadelphia, PA: Chelsea House, 1999.

Stone, Lynn M., *Chihuahuas*. Vero Beach, FL: Rourke Publishing, 2005.

Places to Contact

American Kennel Club (AKC) Headquarters
260 Madison Ave, New York, NY 10016
Telephone: 212-696-8200

On the Web

Visit our Web site for lots of links about Chihuahuas:

http://www.childsworld.com/links

Note to Parents, Teachers, and Librarians: We routinely check our Web links to make sure they're safe, active sites—so encourage your readers to check them out!

Index

About the Author

Susan H. Gray has a Master's degree in zoology. She has written more than 70 science and reference books for children. She loves to garden and play the piano. Susan lives in Cabot, Arkansas, with her husband Michael and many pets.